CAPTURED
TELEVISION
HISTORY

TV BRINGS THE
MOON LANDING TO EARTH

An Augmented Reading Experience

By Rebecca Rissman

Content Adviser: Alan Schroeder, Professor,
School of Journalism, Northeastern University

COMPASS POINT BOOKS
a capstone imprint

Compass Point Books are published by Capstone Press,
1710 Roe Crest Drive, North Mankato, Minnesota 56003
www.capstonepub.com

Editorial Credits
Michelle Bisson, editor; Tracy McCabe, designer; Svetlana Zhurkin, media researcher;
Katy LaVigne, production specialist

Photo Credits
Getty Images: CBS Photo Archive, 31, 35, PhotoQuest, 11, ullstein bild/Quurke, 46; NASA,
cover, 5, 6, 9, 14, 19, 20, 22, 25, 28, 29, 32, 37, 43, 44, 45, 48, 49, 51, 56 (top right and
bottom), 57, 58, 59, Kim Shiflett, 54; Newscom: Universal Images Group/Sovfoto, 26, UPI/Jim
Ruymen, 53, Zuma Press/Photoshot/Uppa, 12; Shutterstock: Aleks49, 17, 56 (top left)

Library of Congress Cataloging-in-Publication Data
Names: Rissman, Rebecca, author.
Title: TV brings the moon landing to Earth / by Rebecca Rissman.
Description: North Mankato, Minnesota : Compass Point Books, [2020] | Series:
4D : an augmented reading experience | Audience: Ages 10-12. | Audience: Grade 4-6.
Identifiers: LCCN 2018054580| ISBN 9780756559991 (hardcover)
ISBN 9780756560034 (pbk.) | ISBN 9780756560072 (ebook pdf)
Subjects: LCSH: Space flight to the moon—Juvenile literature. | Space flight to the moon—
Press coverage—Juvenile literature. | Apollo 11 (Spacecraft)-—Juvenile literature. | Project
Apollo (U.S.)—Juvenile literature. | Space race—United States—History—20th century—
Juvenile literature. | United States—Politics and government—1953-1961—Juvenile literature.
Classification: LCC TL789.8.U6 A581145 2019 | DDC 629.45/4—dc23
LC record available at https://lccn.loc.gov/2018054580

All internet sites in the back matter were available and accessible when this book was
sent to press.

Download the Capstone  app!

- Ask an adult to download the Capstone 4D app.

- Scan the cover and stars inside the book for additional content.

When you scan a spread, you'll find fun extra stuff
to go with this book! You can also find these things
on the web at www.capstone4D.com using the
password: moonlanding.59991

Printed and bound in the United States of America.
PA70

TABLE**OF**CONTENTS

ChapterOne
TENSION

At 4:18 p.m. on July 20, 1969, two astronauts felt the spidery legs of their spacecraft settle onto the surface of the moon. The bleak, stark landing site was called the Sea of Tranquility. It was an ill-suited name for such a spot. It was desolate and dangerous, anything but tranquil—and not even a sea!

Astronaut Neil Armstrong spoke calmly into his headset radio: "Houston," he began. "Tranquility Base here. The *Eagle* has landed."

Almost 245,000 miles (394,300 kilometers) away, NASA's Mission Control Center in Houston, Texas, erupted into cheers. The giant room was filled with row after row of consoles. These were workstations for engineers, doctors, navigation specialists, and technical advisers. Each person had a crucial role to play in keeping the astronauts alive, helping them land on the moon, and then getting them back home to Earth safely.

The crew was radioed by the man sitting behind the Capsule Communication console (CAPCOM). "Roger, Tranquility. We copy you on the ground. You got a bunch of guys about to turn blue. We're breathing again. Thanks a lot."

NASA had just accomplished something amazing. It had sent a crew of astronauts on a mission called

Buzz Aldrin, the second person to walk on the moon, was photographed by Neil Armstrong, the first to do so.

Apollo 11 all the way to the moon. Astronaut Michael Collins remained in a part of the spacecraft called the command module (CM). This orbited around the moon. At the same time, two other astronauts, Neil Armstrong and Buzz Aldrin, rode a lunar module (LM) called *Eagle* down to the surface of the moon.

No humans had ever landed on the moon before. This was an amazing feat of engineering, science, bravery, and creativity. But the crew of Apollo 11 wasn't done yet. Aldrin and Armstrong were about to exit their spacecraft. Then they were going to attempt to walk on the moon.

NASA planned to broadcast live television footage of the first-ever moonwalk. This would serve more than one purpose. First, it would allow people across the globe to share in this historic achievement.

Second, it would prove that a moon landing had, in fact, occurred. Many people at the time doubted that humans could travel to the moon. Video footage would show them that it really happened.

Armstrong and Aldrin were busy in the *Eagle*. They stepped into their bulky spacesuits and went over detailed checklists. They couldn't make any mistakes. As the astronauts got ready to step onto the powdery surface of the moon, a young electrical engineer on Earth quietly panicked. His name was Stan Lebar. He was about to face the most stressful trial of his career. Lebar had created the video camera that would videotape the astronauts' moonwalk. This had been a very difficult task. The camera had to withstand the pressures of launch. It also had to be lightweight. It had to be durable enough to weather the very hot and very cold temperatures found in space.

Lebar didn't just create a video camera for this event. He also developed a special way to transmit the video footage from the moon to Earth. It was a complex process. If everything went well, the astronauts' footage would follow a long, zigzagging course through space. The footage would bounce from the spacecraft's antenna to Earth, then up to satellites, before finally appearing on TV screens around the world. It used brand-new technology. Lebar had tested and retested it, but he couldn't be sure it would work.

People around the world were excited to watch the first moonwalk. In the moments leading up to that event, more than half a billion viewers gathered around TV sets. News stations had devoted hours of airtime to this story. Now everyone waited for the show of a lifetime.

Lebar nervously rubbed his lucky rabbit's foot. If the video footage didn't transmit from the moon, NASA would say it was his fault. If something went wrong, Lebar would have to apologize to a global audience for his failure. His reputation and the hopes of millions of viewers were on the line.

NASA understood how important this mission was to the world. The agency made sure to capture every important moment on videotape. Cameras videotaped the action in Mission Control. One camera was mounted high in the room. Others were carried around by cameramen. This video was sent to news stations to broadcast to their viewers.

The minutes ticked by. Aldrin and Armstrong prepared to open the hatch to their spacecraft. This would expose them to the vacuum of space. The moon had no oxygen to breathe. If their spacesuits weren't perfectly sealed, they would die.

Cameramen zoomed in on the stressed faces of the men in Mission Control and captured the tension in the room. Men studied stacks of papers. They double-checked their math. Their instruments

The cameras used by Stan Lebar were revolutionary at the time of the moon landing.

blinked. The room was hazy with cigarette smoke.

Mission Control was arranged a little like a stadium. Four rows of consoles sat on ascending levels. The back row was the highest. This gave television viewers at home a glimpse of each of the consoles, blinking with electronics, and the men operating them. This setup also gave everyone in Mission Control a clear view of the giant screens mounted on the front wall. In just a few moments, the screens might show the video footage transmitted from the surface of the moon.

The astronauts' radio communication was piped into speakers mounted inside Mission Control. Armstrong's voice crackled over the radio. "The hatch is coming open." Men in Mission Control leaned forward tensely at their consoles. They stared at the blank screen at the front of the room as they listened intently. Would the astronauts survive?

The hatch opened. Both astronauts continued speaking into their radios. They were fine.

Now it was time for the next step. Armstrong would climb out onto the "porch," or ladder, which was outside *Eagle*. Once there, he would tug on a little ring attached to a cord. This would open a small compartment and allow Lebar's camera to tumble into place. Inside *Eagle*, Aldrin would flip a switch to power up the camera.

Lebar's camera would point directly at the porch. This meant it would capture Armstrong's first movements on the moon. If everything went according to plan, the large, blank screen in Mission Control was about to flicker to life with footage from the moon.

Inside NASA's Manned Spacecraft Center, Lebar sweated. On the moon, Armstrong spoke into his microphone: "I'm going to pull [the ring] now." The astronaut grasped the small metal ring and gave it a tug. Lebar's camera dropped perfectly into place.

CAPCOM spoke, "Roger, we copy. We're standing by for your TV."

In many places across the world, people huddled around television sets. No one knew exactly what they would see, or how it would look. As Lebar's camera hummed to life in space, each news network switched

Worldwide, people watched the moon landing broadcast. They often stood together in groups.

away from shots of its anchormen or Mission Control. It was time to watch men walk on the moon.

In Mission Control, a gray line flickered across the huge screen. Then a squiggle.

CAPCOM gasped: "Man, we're getting a picture on the TV."

Television screens across the globe glowed with the same footage. At first the images were hard to understand. They seemed to be upside down. Then the screen flickered and appeared to show the footage in negative. What should have been dark glowed bright white. Finally the picture resolved. A grainy black-and-white video showed an astronaut slowly climbing down a ladder.

Armstrong paused on the ladder's last step.

BROADCASTING TRAGEDY

Viewers watched in real time as President Kennedy's alleged assassin was shot by a man named Jack Ruby.

In the 1960s viewers had witnessed violent events on live television. In 1963 Lee Harvey Oswald assassinated President John F. Kennedy. Later, news crews captured Oswald on live television as he walked to a county jail. While cameras rolled, Oswald was shot and killed by a nightclub owner named Jack Ruby. This was the first time someone had been murdered on live television in the United States.

Today many TV stations insert a small delay between an event and the live television broadcast of it. This gives television producers time to interrupt the broadcast and prevent viewers from seeing something upsetting. NASA did not include a delay in the footage of its moon landing. This meant that if something terrible occurred on the moon, the world would see it happen live.

He was just inches from the surface of the moon. The camera pointed directly at his feet. Armstrong described what he could see. The moon's surface was covered in dust. "It's almost like a powder," he mused. "I'm going to step off the LM now." His voice sounded crackly because it was transmitted from so far away.

On-screen Armstrong seemed to take a big, slow-motion step down. His feet left the last rung of the ladder and sank slowly onto the surface of the moon. Objects on the moon have about one-sixth of the gravity they have on Earth. This means they are pulled toward the surface of the moon with less force. Armstrong's descent from the ladder was the first live footage of someone moving in the reduced gravity of the moon. It was an extraordinary sight.

The astronaut's boots settled into the fine moon dust. Armstrong said, "That's one small step for man, one giant leap for mankind." As Armstrong took his first tentative steps on the moon, newscasters on Earth did their best to narrate the scene. Many struggled to decipher the audio from the footage. On NBC Frank McGee couldn't understand Armstrong's declaration. Had he said, "One small step for man, one giant leap for man"? Static had interrupted the transmission in the middle of Armstrong's statement. Someone had to clarify the wording for him.

On CBS Cronkite was joined by Wally Schirra, an astronaut from earlier NASA missions. Schirra helped explain some of what the astronauts were experiencing. Cronkite's attention soon turned to the fact that the moonwalk was being broadcast.

"Boy, look at those pictures," he exclaimed.

Schirra couldn't get over his excitement at the

"That's one small step for man, one giant leap for mankind."

footage. He said, "Oh, thank you, television for letting us watch this one." Cronkite commented, "Isn't this something? 240,000 miles out there on the moon and we're seeing this history be made."

Armstrong continued exploring the moon. He kicked up some dust and took a few more tentative hops. Soon, he helped Aldrin climb down onto the moon as well.

About 600 million people watched the moon

landing. That was about one-sixth of the total global population at the time. Approximately seven out of every 10 adults in America watched it. Many children watched too. At the time, not everyone owned a television set. This meant that many people had to watch it on a friend or neighbor's TV or gather in public to watch. The broadcast of the moonwalk took place just after 10:30 p.m. Eastern Daylight Time (EDT) in America. In Europe, Asia, and Australia it was very early in the morning, but millions tuned in.

The moon landing is believed to have had more viewers than any previous television broadcast. The three national networks—ABC, NBC, and CBS—all worked hard to ensure that their coverage would be perfect. They paid animators to create footage of spaceships traveling in space. They built mock lunar landers, then paid actors to wear spacesuits and pretend to pilot them. Adding such features to the broadcast helped viewers understand the complex space mission. They also helped to keep viewers interested and engaged. These elaborate productions were expensive. In all, the three news networks spent about $13 million on the broadcast.

As footage streamed through space of Armstrong and Aldrin walking on the moon, one man on Earth sighed happily. Stan Lebar was delighted for NASA. He was also relieved. The camera worked! His camera worked.

ChapterTwo
THE RACE TO THE MOON

On October 4, 1957, the Soviet Union launched the first human-made satellite into space. It was called *Sputnik*. *Sputnik* collected information about Earth's atmosphere. It also recorded the temperature inside the satellite and on its outer surface. *Sputnik* sent this information down to Earth with a beeping signal. By today's standards *Sputnik* was very simple. In 1957, however, it represented a huge advance in technology.

The U.S. and the Soviet Union had been allies in World War II, but their political systems were at odds. In the late 1940s Soviet leaders aggressively expanded their country's communist influence in Eastern Europe. Soviet armed forces, called the Red Army, occupied many countries, including Poland, Hungary, and Bulgaria. The Union of Soviet Socialist Republics (USSR) worked to convert its new territories to communism. Soviet leaders sometimes used violence to accomplish this goal.

For their part, Americans were distrustful of the Soviet Union. They believed communism was wrong. Instead, they thought that capitalism was a better and more sustainable economic and political system. Americans did not like to see communism growing in Eastern Europe.

The relationship between the Soviet Union and

A model of the first *Sputnik* can be viewed in a museum in Moscow, Russia.

the U.S. grew more strained over the years. Each side wanted to show that it was superior. The two world powers worked to develop their militaries and technologies. If war ever broke out between them, each side wanted to be prepared to win. This state of tension was called the Cold War (1945–1991).

When the Soviets launched *Sputnik*, they expanded the Cold War with a battle known as the space race. This was the contest between the U.S. and the Soviet Union to show dominance in space exploration. Each side wanted to advance in space first. At the time many people wondered if humans could live on the moon or other planets. People thought countries might be able to expand into territories out in space. They also feared that weapons would be launched from space. The U.S. and the USSR both wanted to get to space first. This would help them show their power and control.

After *Sputnik* the Soviets continued to enjoy a lead in the space race. On November 3, 1957, the Soviets sent the first animal into space. It was a dog named Laika. On April 12, 1961, a Soviet cosmonaut named Yuri Gagarin became the first human to fly into space in a space capsule called the *Vostok-1*. He flew for 108 minutes and orbited Earth once.

The United States followed with its own small achievements in space. In 1958 President Dwight D. Eisenhower authorized the creation of an American space agency. It was called the National Aeronautics and Space Administration (NASA). NASA hired people to launch satellites. At NASA people also worked on new, powerful rockets. NASA hoped to send a human up into space quickly.

John F. Kennedy became president in 1961. He believed that the U.S. should prioritize space exploration. He thought that a strong space program

Yuri Gagarin's trip into space was front-page news in the U.S.

would boost American spirits. Kennedy and his vice president, Lyndon B. Johnson, were both very excited about stepping up the space race. They encouraged people at NASA to work hard to beat the Soviets.

NASA sent Alan Shepard into space on board
a space capsule called *Freedom 7* on May 5, 1961.
Shepard's mission was a success. However, it was
very short. It lasted just 15 minutes. This was less
than one-seventh of the time Soviet cosmonaut
Gagarin had flown in space. Shepard did not orbit
Earth. He flew in a simple, short arc. The U.S. was
losing the space race.

Twenty days after Shepard's mission, Kennedy
made a speech to Congress. He said, "I believe that
this nation should commit itself to achieving the
goal, before this decade is out, of landing a man on

"I believe that this nation should commit itself to achieving the goal . . . of landing a man on the moon."

the Moon and returning him safely to the Earth." This was a lofty goal. NASA did not yet have the technology, experience, expertise, scientific knowledge, training, or money that would be needed to send a man to the moon.

But NASA soon began developing a plan to accomplish Kennedy's goal. The agency would work toward a moon mission in stages. The first stage, already under way, was called Project Mercury. This was a set of missions using a simple spaceship, or capsule, called *Mercury*. Shepard had ridden a *Mercury* capsule into space.

On February 20, 1962, John Glenn orbited Earth three times in a *Mercury* capsule. His mission showed that NASA was starting to catch up to the Soviets in the space race. TV news covered Glenn's mission breathlessly. News producers switched from coverage of news anchors at their desks to long-distance camera shots of Glenn's rocket on its launchpad. When the countdown reached zero and the rocket lurched into the air, CBS anchor Walter Cronkite couldn't contain his excitement. He yelped, "Go, baby!" The three national networks all aired the launch. More than 40 million people watched.

After Project Mercury, NASA moved on to Project Gemini. These were more complex, two-passenger spacecraft. Gemini spacecraft were able to dock, or pair up, with another spacecraft while in space.

Some Gemini astronauts could exit their capsules and float freely in space—known as a spacewalk. Project Gemini helped NASA develop the skills necessary for a moon mission, which would likely require astronauts to steer, dock, and exit their spaceship.

As the U.S. manned space program advanced, TV also evolved. In the 1960s the three major networks expanded their nightly news programs from 15 to 30 minutes. These broadcasts kept viewers informed of current events.

TV news networks also cut into other programs during times of crisis. On November 22, 1963, daytime television viewers were startled to see their programs interrupted. Journalists appeared on each of the networks with a troubling announcement. President Kennedy had been shot. Viewers watched, rapt, as the story developed. They eventually learned that the president had been killed. Vice President Johnson would assume the presidency. Allowing the news to break into other programming showed that the news was urgent and important.

In the 1960s the topics covered by TV news broadcasts were often very controversial. The Vietnam War, for example, was an event that was widely covered on television, and that divided the nation. Video footage showed graphic glimpses of the battlegrounds in Vietnam, and then covered antiwar protests in the U.S. Many did not agree about what to do in Vietnam. Some wanted the United States to leave the conflict, while others wanted it to stay and fight. The nightly news highlighted this divide.

Television news producers thought that the U.S. space program could unite the country. Networks dedicated themselves to covering NASA's space missions. These exciting spectacles were a welcome relief from controversial news. News segments focusing on NASA's early space missions gave Americans the chance to unite in support of the nation's astronauts and in their desire to win the space race by beating the Soviets to the moon.

TV news crews worked hard to create dynamic coverage of NASA's missions. They invited expert guests to appear on camera. They also often extended their air time. Astronauts sometimes sat next to news anchors on camera. They helped explain the science and excitement of these missions to the public.

But before NASA accomplished its first spacewalk, the Soviets swooped in with another victory. On March 18, 1965, Soviet cosmonaut Alexei Leonov exited his spacecraft while orbiting Earth. He performed a 12-minute spacewalk. The Soviets televised this event. Soviet viewers watched with delight as Leonov floated in space.

Three months later, astronaut Ed White performed the first U.S. spacewalk from a Gemini capsule. His 23-minute spacewalk was broadcast on television. As White floated in space, he exclaimed, "I feel like a million dollars!"

After Gemini, NASA moved forward with its next phase, Project Apollo. Engineers hoped that Apollo would bring NASA's astronauts to the moon. Landing a spaceship on the moon was incredibly complicated. But what made it even more difficult was that NASA also wanted to get the spaceship home. This meant they had to design a spacecraft to fly to the moon, land, and take off again.

NASA came up with a complicated plan for Project Apollo. It was called Lunar Orbit Rendezvous

"I feel like a million dollars!"

In 1965 astronaut Ed White made history with the first U.S. spacewalk.

(LOR). This involved sending a three-part spacecraft into space. One part was the command module (CM). This held a cockpit big enough for three astronauts. Another component was called the service module. This held the main power supply and oxygen the astronauts needed. The last component was called the lunar module (LM). This was a small spacecraft with its own engines. Two astronauts could climb into it and separate from the rest of their craft.

SOVIET SECRETS

Alexei Leonov made history with his spacewalk. The unknown story is that he almost died doing so.

Few people knew that Alexei Leonov nearly died at the end of his spacewalk. His spacesuit had become overfilled with oxygen. He struggled to move his arms and legs. His hands slipped out of his gloves. His boots stretched away from his feet. Leonov needed to climb back into his spacecraft. This was impossible in his balloon-like suit. Leonov did something dangerous and drastic. He opened a valve in his suit. This released oxygen out into space. It partially deflated his suit, but it could have killed him. If too much oxygen drained out, he would have died from a lack of the vital gas. But Leonov got lucky. He climbed back into his spacecraft alive.

This information was not released until after the fall of the Soviet Union. Before that the Soviets tried hard to show a perfect image of their space program. They did not want anyone to know about their problems.

The LM's small engines were powerful enough to move it through space. When they were ready, the astronauts in the LM could reconnect, or dock, with the rest of their spacecraft.

LOR was NASA's best shot at a moon landing. But it was still very risky. It required the team of three astronauts to split up. One would remain in the CM. He would orbit the moon. The two others would fly down to the surface of the moon in the LM. When they were ready, they would use a small engine on the LM to launch themselves back up into space. Then the CM and LM would have to meet up perfectly in space to dock. After that all three astronauts would sit in the CM cockpit. They would fire a series of powerful engines. These would send them back to Earth.

Project Apollo utilized many brand-new technologies. Much of what NASA was attempting to do was not yet understood. No one knew exactly what awaited the astronauts on the moon. Some people thought that they might find aliens there. Others worried that the moon would be toxic. They feared that the astronauts would die.

Though President Kennedy had died, the space program still worked to meet his goal of landing a man on the moon by 1970. President Johnson led the charge, urging NASA to work quickly and lobbying Congress to provide the necessary funding. Despite Johnson's support, NASA could not build everything it needed on its own. So, NASA hired a company to build the command and service modules for the Apollo mission. Some of the astronauts worried that the first Apollo capsules hadn't been constructed well.

Astronaut Gus Grissom was scheduled to fly on the first Apollo mission. This mission would test out the Apollo spacecraft. Grissom said the spacecraft was a lemon. This meant that he thought it was unsafe. NASA engineers worked hard to fix all of its problems, but Grissom was pessimistic. The day he left for the

launch rehearsal, Grissom picked a lemon from a tree in his yard. His wife asked him why he'd done it and Grissom responded, "I'm going to hang it on that spacecraft." Grissom never returned home.

On January 27, 1967, Grissom and two other crew members, Ed White and Roger Chaffee, climbed into their Apollo command module. They were practicing for an upcoming launch. A wire sparked inside their spacecraft and a fire started. Inside the command module, the astronauts breathed 100 percent oxygen. This is a very flammable gas. Many things inside

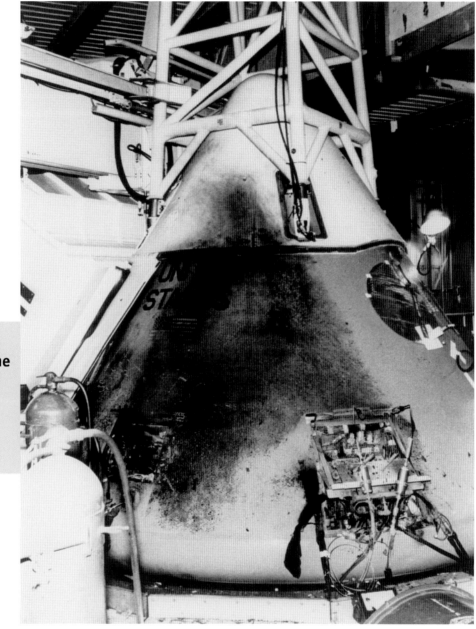

The intense heat of the fire that killed the Apollo 1 astronauts can even be seen on the outside of the damaged command module.

the command module were made from flammable materials. An explosive fire erupted. The astronauts were trapped. All three men died within moments. This tragedy reminded Americans that spaceflight was still very dangerous.

But the danger of spaceflight wasn't the only obstacle NASA had to overcome in its mission to get humans to the moon. There was also a growing public reluctance to fund the expensive agency. In 1961, when Kennedy challenged NASA to land a man on the moon, many Americans were excited by the idea. However, as years passed, some people grew weary of the expensive space agency. NASA was paid for out of the federal budget. In total, the Apollo program would cost the U.S. government more than $25 billion. People at NASA wanted to show Americans that the work and money they had put into the space program was worth it. They knew that a television broadcast of the moon landing would help to show everyone what their money had paid for.

Televising the moon landing also required new technology. Regular movie cameras weighed as much as 700 pounds (317 kilograms) and used a lot of power to run. NASA needed small, lightweight, energy-efficient cameras to bring into space. Stan Lebar worked for five years to create the right camera for space missions. A team of 75 engineers helped. The camera was very impressive. It weighed 7 pounds (3.17 kg) and used just 7 watts of electricity. The camera was also durable. It could survive the extreme temperatures of space. That meant it would still work between minus 250 and 300 degrees Fahrenheit (minus 157 and 184 degrees Celsius).

It could also capture images in the bright sun and dark shadows of the moon. Lebar gave NASA the perfect tool to capture the moon landing. Now NASA just had to get its astronauts to the moon.

Project Apollo proceeded quickly. NASA launched the first crewed mission, Apollo 7, in October 1968. And then, in December 1968, Apollo 8 orbited the moon.

Richard M. Nixon was inaugurated as president in January 1969. He was eager to see the U.S. succeed in the space race. He watched excitedly as Apollo 9 launched in March, and Apollo 10 followed in May.

CBS news anchor Walter Cronkite taped a program on Apollo 8 at the Hayden Planetarium in New York.

These missions helped astronauts practice the skills they needed for a moon landing. By the summer of 1969, NASA was ready to try to land the crew of Apollo 11 on the moon.

Deke Slayton, Chief of the Astronaut Office, chose the crew. Slayton had a motto: "Any crew can fly any mission." This meant that any NASA astronaut with the right training and background could succeed in any mission to which he was assigned.

For Apollo 11 Slayton chose Michael Collins, an experienced Air Force pilot and Gemini astronaut, to be the command module pilot. This role required excellent flight skills and attention to detail. For the lunar module pilot, Slayton chose Buzz Aldrin.

"Any crew can fly any mission."

Aldrin was an Air Force pilot and Gemini astronaut with a PhD in aeronautics and astronautics. Slayton named Neil Armstrong as the mission's commander. Armstrong, now a civilian, was a former naval aviator and test pilot. He had a degree in engineering and had commanded Gemini 8.

Armstrong, Aldrin, and Collins trained for seven months. Though Armstrong and Aldrin would walk on the moon, Collins was not disappointed by his assignment. He knew that his role flying the command module around the moon by himself was crucial. He also looked forward to achieving a space first of his own. He would become the first human to orbit the moon by himself.

As the launch date for Apollo 11 approached, people at NASA argued about who would be the first man to walk on the moon. Aldrin thought it should be him. In Gemini flights, the pilot, not the commander, left the spacecraft. But Slayton thought that the senior astronaut should get the honor. Armstrong had been at NASA for one year longer than Aldrin. Also, the LM's door to the outside was on Armstrong's side. The astronauts' bulky spacesuits meant it would be hard for Aldrin to climb over Armstrong to make his exit. In the end, NASA decided: Armstrong would be first.

Now all NASA had to do was get its crew to the moon. And bring them home again.

ChapterThree
THE MISSION

On July 16, 1969, news anchor Walter Cronkite sat behind his CBS news desk. A countdown to the launch of Apollo 11 played across the bottom of the screen. Cronkite told his viewers all about the upcoming mission. Apollo 11 would launch using powerful rockets. Then it would loop around Earth once. After that it would fire a rocket to thrust it toward the moon.

When the countdown reached zero, Apollo 11's rockets blasted it off the launchpad. Cronkite could hardly contain himself. "Oh boy. Oh, boy, it looks good," he exclaimed. The spacecraft zoomed up into the sky. It traveled faster and faster. The television camera crews struggled to keep it in their frames.

In addition to Cronkite and his guest commentator, astronaut Wally Schirra, several voices from inside Mission Control at NASA were audible to the TV audience. NASA allowed news stations to access some of its radio communications. This helped Americans feel connected to their space program.

This decision to allow the public to hear its communications was unusual. Before this, many U.S. agencies were very private. Emergencies were sometimes reported only after they had occurred. Even then, many agencies released little information

Astronaut Wally Schirra (left) and news anchor Walter Cronkite talked on the field before the launch of Apollo 11.

to the public. NASA was different. It allowed journalists to sit in a special section of Mission Control. They were allowed to watch events from this important room as they happened. NASA also released the record of its communication with its space crews after the flights. This was partly in response to the secretive Soviet space program. The Soviets often kept their space missions a secret until after they were complete. By being open with the public, NASA stood out as different.

Meanwhile, as Apollo 11 began its long journey to the moon, most regular television programming resumed. Viewers were updated on Apollo 11's progress every night on the news shows.

The astronauts sent short TV broadcasts down to Earth. News stations picked up these videos and played them for their audiences. The videos let viewers know what the astronauts were doing. They also provided an interesting glimpse into life in space. On July 17 Michael Collins showed TV viewers the astronauts' neatly packaged, freeze-dried food. On July 18 Armstrong and Aldrin sent a short video as they floated around in their spacesuits. As the moon landing grew nearer, news networks devoted more and more time to the upcoming event.

On July 19 Apollo 11 was coming close to the moon. A set of rockets on the spacecraft fired. These knocked it into orbit around the moon. The astronauts had been in space for almost 76 hours. It was almost time for them to attempt the first-ever moon landing.

On Sunday, July 20, 1969, CBS began its marathon coverage. CBS planned to devote 31 straight hours to the event, boasting that the moon landing would be "a most historic event, but our own coverage will be up to matching it." Newscasters on all three networks informed their viewers of exactly what was happening in space. They told them that the crew on board Apollo 11 was looping around the moon. They were almost 245,000 miles (394,300 km) from Earth.

Around noon, Houston time, the crew of Apollo 11 was ready to reach the moon. It was time to separate

Eagle—the lunar module—was photographed in space from the command module, *Columbia*.

the different parts of the spacecraft. Astronauts Neil Armstrong and Buzz Aldrin climbed into *Eagle*. Collins stayed in the command module, *Columbia*. He would keep orbiting the moon while Aldrin and Armstrong traveled down to the moon's surface. At 12:18 p.m. Armstrong and Aldrin were buckled into the cockpit of *Eagle*. Collins pushed a button in his cockpit. This sent *Eagle* floating out into space. As the LM drifted away. Collins told the two, "Okay, there you go! Beautiful!" Armstrong used a set of controls on his side of the LM cockpit to steady *Eagle*.

The two spacecraft looped around the moon once

together. Collins double-checked that his command module was working perfectly. He needed to be sure he would be able to meet up with *Eagle* after the moon landing. Aldrin and Armstrong were busy in *Eagle*. They worked quickly to prepare for their trip to the moon's surface.

Soon, *Eagle*'s engines fired. These sent Aldrin and Armstrong down toward the moon. Much of *Eagle*'s flight was controlled by computer. This device used radar to sense where to send the spacecraft.

TV viewers who tuned in to CBS watched an animated version of *Eagle* descending through space. Orange flames shot from its engines. Just below it was a large clock counting down until the anticipated time of the moon landing. The voices of the astronauts, Mission Control, Cronkite, and Schirra all narrated the scene. Occasionally a set of numbers flashed over the animation. These described *Eagle*'s speed, height, and distance to the moon to give viewers the feeling that they were fully informed about the mission. Of course, TV viewers could really see only prerecorded animated images. The images did not match the exact progress of *Eagle*'s actual descent, which they could not see.

In fact, as Schirra and Cronkite spoke calmly to their television viewers about the astronauts' mission, Aldrin and Armstrong experienced an emergency on board *Eagle*. It is clearly audible on the news

"What's this alarm, Wally?"

broadcast. But since Schirra and Cronkite didn't know what was happening, they did not inform their viewers. Therefore, few people understood exactly what was going on.

While Aldrin and Armstrong approached the moon, an alarm rang out inside *Eagle*. Aldrin had never heard this type of alarm before. He wondered what it meant. Armstrong's voice snapped over the radio: "Program alarm!" Cronkite and Schirra continued to narrate the footage casually and confidently. They joked a little and reminded their viewers that the moon landing was minutes away.

On the ground, people in Mission Control scrambled to understand *Eagle*'s alarm. A computer expert in Mission Control thought that the LM's computer was overloaded. It could not handle all the information it was processing. The alarm simply alerted the crew of this. He thought the men should still try to land on the moon. Mission Control told the astronauts: "We're go on that alarm." In other words, they could continue their mission.

The alarm rang out again. This time Cronkite paid attention. "What's this alarm, Wally?" Schirra explained that it had to do with the computers on board *Eagle*, but that the crew was still "Go." His voice sounded calm.

News networks occasionally switched away from their anchors or the animated *Eagle*. They showed crowds at airports, at Disneyland, or on the street watching the footage of the moon landing. This contributed to the feeling that the whole world was watching.

Eagle dropped down toward the surface of the moon. At 3,000 feet (914 meters) CAPCOM told the crew: "You're GO for landing." As *Eagle* descended, more alarms rang out inside the ship. The lunar module's computer was still having trouble handling all of the information it was processing. The astronauts reported these alarms to Mission Control, but again, Cronkite and Schirra ignored them. They focused instead on their excitement at the upcoming moon landing. Mission Control told the crew they were still clear to land.

Armstrong expertly steered *Eagle* toward a flat, safe landing place. News networks continued to play the astronauts' radio communications to Mission Control. These were technical readings from their instruments. They meant little to the average viewer. To keep things exciting, the stations switched to animated moons and actors wearing spacesuits pretending to fly spacecraft.

But news anchors and their guests fell silent as the astronauts closed in on the moon. It seemed as though they didn't want to interrupt this historic moment with their own narration. They simply let their viewers listen to the technical communications between the astronauts and Mission Control.

"You're GO for landing."

"You guys are getting prime TV time!"

It took longer than expected for Armstrong to land *Eagle*. This meant that ABC's animation showed a moon lander touching down minutes before the actual *Eagle* made contact with the moon's surface. While Armstrong and Aldrin coasted over its surface, ABC viewers watched footage of actors dressed as astronauts inside a mock cockpit. Then the screen switched back to the animated lander resting on the surface of the moon. When Armstrong finally lowered *Eagle* expertly onto the surface of the moon at 4:17 p.m. EDT, ABC showed the animated LM touching down once again.

Shortly after bringing *Eagle* down onto the moon, Armstrong shut down his engines and looked at Aldrin. The two men smiled at each other. They had done it! They clasped bulky, gloved hands for a moment.

Armstrong and Aldrin had planned to wait on the surface of the moon for several hours before leaving *Eagle*. But both men were ready to explore. They radioed Mission Control to ask if they could take their moonwalk five hours earlier than planned. CAPCOM responded immediately that they could: "You guys are getting prime TV time!"

Armstrong and Aldrin suited up. They snapped their airtight helmets and gloves onto their thick spacesuits. These would protect them from the harsh environment on the moon. Finally, at 9:28 p.m. EDT, they opened *Eagle*'s door. Outside, they saw the gray, rocky surface of the moon. Armstrong pulled on a cord that let a video camera fall into place on the outside of *Eagle*. Aldrin flipped a switch to activate it.

The camera started rolling. It transmitted an electronic signal to tracking stations in Australia and California. In Australia the signal was converted into video. This video signal then went back up into space to satellites. The satellites bounced the video down to Mission Control in Houston. Finally, from there, the video went out to news networks. This was a long and complex path for the signal. It, along with the smaller bandwidth size, reduced the quality of the video. Though the original footage was crisp, what made it to televisions on Earth was grainy and looked blurry.

Armstrong took his first shaky steps on the moon at 9:39 p.m. EDT. Then Aldrin joined him. The men collected rock samples. They hopped around and joked a little. Armstrong set up a tripod about 40 feet (12 m) from *Eagle*. He then took the camera from the outside of *Eagle* and set it on top of the tripod. This expanded the view for their television audiences. Instead of just pointing at the side of their LM, it now showed a wide view of the moon.

Newscasters remained mostly silent during the moonwalk. They let TV viewers listen to the

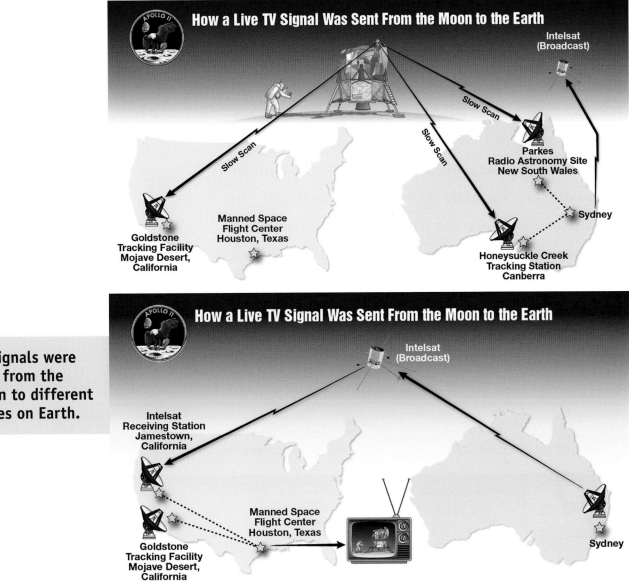

How a Live TV Signal Was Sent From the Moon to the Earth

Intelsat
(Broadcast)

Slow Scan

Slow Scan

Parkes
Radio Astronomy Site
New South Wales

Sydney

Slow Scan

Goldstone
Tracking Facility
Mojave Desert,
California

Manned Space
Flight Center
Houston, Texas

Honeysuckle Creek
Tracking Station
Canberra

How a Live TV Signal Was Sent From the Moon to the Earth

Intelsat
(Broadcast)

Intelsat
Receiving Station
Jamestown,
California

Manned Space
Flight Center
Houston, Texas

Goldstone
Tracking Facility
Mojave Desert,
California

Sydney

TV signals were sent from the moon to different places on Earth.

astronauts and the crews in Mission Control. Occasionally text would flash across the video with messages such as "LIVE FROM THE SURFACE OF THE MOON." This helped viewers who had just tuned in know exactly what they were seeing.

Aldrin and Armstrong planted a U.S. flag on the

moon. Because there is no wind on the moon, the flagpole included a horizontal bar to keep the flag unfurled. The two men stood back to look at it. Just then a voice crackled into their headset radios. It was President Richard Nixon. He wanted to talk to them.

Television screens on Earth showed Nixon sitting at his desk. Occasionally the image split to show both the president and the astronauts on the moon. Holding a phone to one ear, Nixon told them that their moonwalk was uniting everyone on the planet. "For one priceless moment, in the whole history of man, all the people on this earth are truly one. One in their pride in what you have done." Armstrong thanked the president. He said, "It's a great honor and privilege for us to be here, representing not only the United States but men of peace of all nations . . . men with a

Aldrin and Armstrong planted the U.S. flag on the moon— winning that part of the space race.

THE LOST MOON LANDING VIDEOTAPES

NASA Archive   2009 Restoration

These stills show the moon landing footage before and after the restoration of the videotapes.

During the moon landing NASA recorded the raw video footage sent from *Apollo 11*. This footage had not yet been converted to the smaller bandwidth. This meant that it was much clearer than what television viewers saw. The images were crisper and easier to understand.

In 2004 historians began to look for this original footage. It had been recorded on tapes of magnetic film. The historians could not find it. In 2006 NASA acknowledged that the footage was probably gone.

To save money back in the 1970s and 1980s NASA reused its magnetic tapes. The agency believed it was likely that the moon landing video had been erased so that the tapes could be reused for another purpose.

Video technicians have worked to restore the footage that was broadcast back in 1969. They carefully removed static and made the images as crisp as possible. These restored videos offer a better view of what the first moon landing was really like.

vision for the future."

Finally, after two and a half hours, the astronauts returned to *Eagle*. They rested inside the small cockpit and prepared to reunite with the command

module. At 12:54 p.m. EDT on Monday July 21, 1969, a set of rockets fired underneath *Eagle*. These launched it off the surface of the moon. *Eagle* soon started orbiting the moon. Four hours later Collins watched as *Eagle* approached his command module. Armstrong expertly flew *Eagle*. The spacecraft docked perfectly. Collins was glad to see his friends again.

Soon the three astronauts gathered in the command module. *Eagle* was not built to withstand the journey back through Earth's atmosphere. The astronauts did not need it anymore. Collins flipped a switch to separate the command module from the LM. Then, *Eagle* went out into space.

On Thursday, July 22, the astronauts fired their engines again. This time the thrust sent them back toward Earth. The three astronauts safely splashed down into the Pacific Ocean on Thursday, July 24, 1969.

ChapterFour
A LASTING IMPACT

The Apollo 11 mission lasted eight days. Neil Armstrong and Buzz Aldrin's moonwalk took just two and a half hours. But thanks in no small part to the extensive TV coverage of this event, its significance has endured.

NASA has estimated that more than one half of the entire global population was aware of the moon landing. In addition to the 600 million people who watched it on live television, others listened to it on the radio. Still others saw footage of it later. Many read about it in newspapers or magazines.

America's Cold War enemy, the Soviet Union, tried to block broadcasts of the moon landing. But many Soviet citizens still found out about it. Some people thought that, with the U.S. landing on the moon, the space race was over. Others disagreed. The Soviets didn't give up. They sent un-crewed lunar landers to the moon. But their program was very expensive and plagued by faulty rockets and equipment. Eventually the Soviets abandoned their goal of landing a human on the moon. Instead, the Soviet space agency switched gears. It focused on other space missions, such as Earth-orbiting space stations.

President Nixon greeted the astronauts after they returned to Earth. He told them, "This is the greatest

week in the history of the world since Creation."
A big part of what made the moon mission so
important was that NASA shared it with the world.
People living across the globe were able to watch the
event as it happened. Many people believed that this
experience connected them.

The moon landing united people who were excited
about space travel. One French scholar remarked on
the mission's incredible impact: "Americans reached
out and touched the moon. But it was a victory for the
indomitable spirit of every man."

Apollo 17 astronaut Gene Cernan test-drove the lunar rover on the moon.

In the years after Apollo 11, NASA sent five additional crews to the moon. Astronauts on these missions walked on the moon. Some drove a simple car called a rover across the lunar surface. They did science experiments. Over time, the public's excitement about space travel faded. Fewer viewers tuned in to watch the missions' televised broadcasts. Project Apollo ended in 1972. In 1975 the U.S. and Soviets launched a cooperative space mission called Apollo-Soyuz. Three American astronauts met up with two Soviet cosmonauts in space. They docked their spacecraft together and shook hands. This joint mission marked the unofficial end of the space race.

Though the initial excitement over the moon landing faded, its video footage remains important. The moon landing video has been reused and repurposed many times. Filmmakers have included clips from the moon landing in documentaries about space travel. Artists have used the footage for video art installations. Other artists have painted still images from the video footage. Famous pop artist Andy Warhol created a series of silkscreens in 1987 called *Moonwalk*. They show Buzz Aldrin standing next to the U.S. flag. Warhol painted each in different vibrant colors. In 2016 a set of two *Moonwalk* prints sold in London, England, for £185,000 ($251,880).

Some artists evoke the importance of the moon landing without using any of the visual images at all. Artist On Kawara creates large black-and-white paintings that show important dates. In Kawara's Today series, three paintings are hung next to one another. They read *July 16, 1969*; *July 20, 1969*; and *July 21, 1969*. Beneath and beside the paintings are boxes filled with newspapers. Headlines declaring "Man Walks on Moon" explain the dates to viewers. Kawara's art assumes that the moon landing is important enough that just seeing the dates will evoke emotions in those who look at the paintings.

The moon landing also inspired books and poetry. Writers had mixed opinions about sending humans to the moon. Some were thrilled. Others were wary.

WAS THE MOON LANDING A HOAX?

The U.S. flag is propped up with a clearly visible horizontal bar.

In the 1960s the idea that humans could land on the moon was hard for many people to understand. Some doubted that it was possible. After Apollo 11 made it to the moon, a small number of people believed that the mission had been faked. They thought that NASA had worked with a movie studio to create the footage broadcast on television news.

In 1969 the idea that the moon landing was fake, or a hoax, was unpopular. Polls showed that fewer than 5 percent of people "doubted the moon voyage had taken place." Over time, however, that number has grown. A 2004 poll showed that 27 percent of Americans between the ages of 18 and 24 "expressed doubts that NASA went to the moon."

People who do not believe that Apollo 11 made it to the moon make several arguments. They note that the U.S. flag planted on the moon should not appear to fly, as it does on film, because the moon has no wind.

This is true. But the flag does not fly. It is propped up with a horizontal bar. Others have suggested that the shadows visible on the moon do not look natural. They believe they were created by stage lighting in a movie studio. NASA has explained that these shadows were created by the special camera lenses and sloping terrain of the moon.

Several Apollo astronauts have struggled to accept that people doubt their accomplishments. Harrison Schmitt, Apollo 17 astronaut, has said, "If people decide they're going to deny the facts of history and the facts of science and technology, there's not much you can do with them. For most of them, I just feel sorry that we failed in their education." In 2002 Buzz Aldrin was confronted by a man who thought he faked his moonwalk. The man called Aldrin "a coward, a liar, and a thief." Aldrin, then 72, punched the man in the face.

British poet W.H. Auden was thankful that the astronauts did not spoil the moon. One month after the Apollo 11 mission, he penned a poem called "Moon Landing" with the words "Unsmudged, thank God, my Moon still queens the Heavens."

The video footage of the moon landing has had a lasting impact on popular culture. One of the most obvious examples of this comes from the MTV network. The creators of MTV wanted unique animation for their new music network. They hired a graphic design firm to create the animation, headed by a designer named Pat Gorman. Gorman and her team used footage from the moon landing in the animation. It showed the astronauts planting the U.S. flag on the moon. Instead of the stars and stripes, they modified the video footage to show flashing, multicolored patterns on the flag. Gorman said, "We thought, 'We're like the guys landing on the moon and claiming it. We claim this land for music.'"

MTV aired its first broadcast in 1981. It opened with the famous moon landing animation. MTV played this animation at the beginning of every hour of programming for its first five years. This exposed a new generation of viewers to this famous video.

Footage from the moon landing has made its way into many different elements of pop culture. A 1992 episode of *The Simpsons* used the audio from the moon landing in a flashback. In it, Homer Simpson's

"We're like the guys landing on the moon and claiming it. We claim this land for music."

Kendrick Lamar won six MTV awards in 2017. The trophies each show an astronaut holding the flag, a tribute to Apollo 11.

dad watches the news footage while Homer sits nearby, ignoring the event.

Other shows have not used the exact footage but have recalled the story of the broadcast itself. *Futurama* and *Doctor Who* have both featured the moon landing broadcast in episodes. Movies have also relied on the story of the Apollo 11 mission. *Transformers: Dark of the Moon*, *Men in Black 3*, and many other films have recalled this mission. In 2018 a movie called *First Man* was released, focusing on Neil Armstrong and his trip to the moon.

The moon landing is also featured in many video

The space program continues, with future trips planned for missions as far away as Mars.

games. Several have included recreations of the original televised footage. *Lego Marvel Super Heroes*, *Kerbal Space Program*, and *Command & Conquer: Yuri's Revenge* all reference the event.

Though the footage from the moon landing is five decades old, it remains an important part of modern culture. This is because it continues to appear in new art, television, and video games. As new artists reuse and manipulate the footage, they add their own spin onto the way it exists in the world.

The first time the world saw Apollo 11's television broadcast, it represented a huge technological leap for humanity. Not only were men walking on the moon, but they were also broadcasting it live. Modern viewers see the video differently. They notice the poor quality of the footage, the crackly audio, the blurry pictures. This changes the way they interpret what they see. Modern viewers also realize that many advances in space occurred after the first moon landing. Today space agencies are preparing for new trips to the moon. They are also working toward a mission to Mars.

As NASA and other space agencies work to explore new frontiers in space, the importance of the first moon landing will not be diminished. The video footage of the landing, and the impression it made on a generation of worldwide viewers, will continue to hold a significant place in history.

Timeline

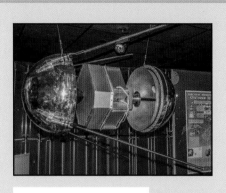

October 4, 1957

Scientists in the Soviet Union launch the first human-made satellite into Earth's orbit. It is called *Sputnik*.

April 12, 1961

Soviet cosmonaut Yuri Gagarin becomes the first human to fly in space. He orbits Earth once.

February 20, 1962

John Glenn becomes the first American to orbit Earth.

November 22, 1963

Lee Harvey Oswald assassinates President John F. Kennedy in Dallas, Texas.

May 1961–May 1963

NASA launches six missions during Project Mercury.

May 5, 1961

Alan Shepard becomes the first American to fly in space. His mission lasts a little more than 15 minutes.

May 25, 1961

President John F. Kennedy makes a speech to a joint session of Congress in which he says, "I believe that this nation should commit itself to achieving the goal, before this decade is out, of landing a man on the moon and returning him safely to Earth."

March 1965–November 1966

NASA launches 10 missions during Project Gemini.

February 3, 1966

Soviet spacecraft *Luna 9* makes an unmanned lunar landing and transmits images of the moon's surface back to Earth.

Timeline

January 27, 1967

The crew of Apollo 1 dies in a fire during a launch rehearsal.

October 1968–December 1972

NASA launches 11 missions during Project Apollo.

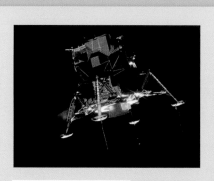

July 21, 1969

Eagle leaves the moon and reunites with the command module, *Columbia*.

July 24, 1969

Apollo 11 crew safely splash into the Pacific Ocean.

July 16, 1969

Apollo 11 launches from Cape Canaveral, Florida.

July 20, 1969

Apollo 11's lunar module, *Eagle*, lands on the moon. Neil Armstrong and Buzz Aldrin take their first moonwalk. It is broadcast around the world.

August 1, 1981

MTV's first moments on television show used footage from Apollo 11.

2018

The movie *First Man* uses footage of the Apollo 11 launch and moon landing.

August 1969

W.H. Auden publishes a poem called "Moon Landing."

Glossary

anchor—the person who presents the news during a television news program

broadcast—to send out a program over the radio or on television

command module—the part of a spacecraft that can support human life during launch and reentry

console—a cabinet or desk containing the equipment necessary for a certain job

dock—to join two spacecraft in space

gravity—the force that attracts objects toward Earth or other bodies with mass

hoax—a trick to make people believe something that is not real

lunar module—the part of a spacecraft that can be used to fly down to the moon, land, and take off again

orbit—the path an object takes as it moves around a celestial body

satellite—a human-made object placed in orbit around the Earth, moon, or other celestial body

tripod—a three-legged stand used to hold a camera

watt—unit used to measure electrical power

Additional Resources

Further Reading

Adamson, Thomas K. *Apollo 11 Moon Landing: An Interactive Space Exploration Adventure.* Mankato, MN: Capstone, 2017.

Berman, Garry. *For the First Time on Television.* Albany, GA: Bear Manor Media, 2016.

Cunningham, Darryl. *How to Fake a Moon Landing: Exposing the Myths of Science Denial.* New York: Abrams, 2013.

Hamby, Rachel. *Televisions* (How It Works). Mendota Heights, MN: North Star Editions, 2017.

Internet Sites

Experience the Apollo 11 Lunar Landing
https://www.firstmenonthemoon.com

NASA: Lunar Landing Sites Selected
https://www.nasa.gov/feature/50-years-ago-lunar-landing-sites-selected

NASA: July 20, 1969: One Giant Leap for Mankind
https://www.nasa.gov/mission_pages/apollo/apollo11.html

Critical Thinking Questions

Consider the challenges facing NASA in its quest to bring a human to the moon. How do you think televising each step toward the moon landing helped the agency? How did it make things more difficult?

How did television news stations play up NASA launches? What did they do to enhance their broadcasts? Use evidence from the text to support your answer.

One reason NASA televised the moon landing was to provide people with evidence that it had actually occurred. How have people used the footage from the moon landing to argue that it was a hoax?

Source Notes

p. 4, "Houston...Tranquility Base here..." "Historic Mission Control," *SpaceCenter. org*, https://spacecenter.org/attractions/ nasa-tram-tour/historic-mission-control/ Accessed April 20, 2018

p. 4, "Roger, Tranquility..." Ibid.

p. 11, "Man, we're getting..." "Man Walks on Another World," *NationalGeographic.com*, http://ngm. nationalgeographic.com/print/1969/12/ moon-landing/astronauts-text Accessed April 20, 2018.

p. 12, "It's almost like a powder..." Ibid.

p. 13, "That's one small step..." Ibid.

p. 14, "Oh, thank you..." "Apollo 11 Part 27, CBS News Coverage of the Moon Walk," August 18, 2010, https://www. youtube.com/watch?v=XisDvCTww4M Accessed April 20, 2018.

pp. 20–21, "I believe that this nation..." "The Moon Decision," *AirandSpace. si.edu*, https://airandspace.si.edu/ exhibitions/apollo-to-the-moon/online/ racing-to-space/moon-decision.cfm Accessed April 20, 2018.

p. 21, "Go, baby!" John Glenn Launch, Walter Cronkite 'Go, Baby!' Live on TV, CBS, February 20, 1962," *Youtube.com*, November 5, 2011, https://www.youtube. com/watch?v=GVB5dg7XX_g Accessed April 20, 2018.

p. 24, "I feel like a million dollars!" Bob Evans, "To Swim in Space: The World's First Spacewalk (Part 2)." *AmericaSpace.com*, http://www.americaspace. com/2014/03/09/to-swim-in-space-the- worlds-first-spacewalk-part-2/ Accessed April 20, 2018.

p. 28, "I'm going to hang it..." https:// history.nasa.gov/Apollo204/zorn/ grissom.htm Accessed April 20, 2018.

p. 34, "Oh boy..." "Launch of Apollo 11 (CBS)," *Youtube.com*, April 1, 2010, https://www.youtube.com/ watch?v=TmHABUfjYPI Accessed April 20, 2018.

p. 36, "... a most historic event..." Steve Knoll, "First Man on the Moon Has the Networks in Orbit," *Variety.com*, July 16, 1969, http://variety.com/1969/biz/news/ first-man-on-the-moon-has-tv-networks- in-orbit-1201342630/ Accessed April 20, 2018.

p. 39, "Program alarm..." "CBS Coverage of Apollo 11 Lunar Landing," *Youtube. com*, July 17, 2014, https://www.youtube. com/watch?v=E96EPhqT-ds Accessed April 30, 2018.

p. 39, "We're go on that alarm. ..." Ibid.

p. 40, "You're GO for landing..." Andrew Chaikin, *A Man on the Moon*. New York: Penguin, 2007, *p.* 196.

p. 41, "You guys are getting..." Ibid., *p.* 204.

p. 43, "LIVE FROM THE SURFACE ..." CBS Coverage of Apollo 11 Lunar Landing, "*Youtube.com*, July 17, 2014, https://www.youtube.com/ watch?v=E96EPhqT-ds Accessed April 20, 2018.

pp. 47–48, ""This is the greatest week..." "Apollo 11 and the World." *AirandSpace. Si.edu*, July 15, 2009, https://airandspace. si.edu/stories/editorial/apollo-11-and- world Accessed April 20, 2018.

p. 48, "Americans reached out ..." "Man on the Moon: 45 Years Later, Remembering Apollo 11," *USNews.com*, July 21, 2014, https://www.usnews.com/ news/articles/2014/07/21/man-on-the- moon-45-years-later-remembering-the- apollo-11-moon-landing Accessed April 20, 2018.

p. 51, "...expressed doubts..." "Why Do People Persist in Denying the Moon Landings?" *AirandSpace.si.edu*, April 1, 2010 https://airandspace.si.edu/stories/ editorial/why-do-people-persist-denying- moon-landings Accessed April 20, 2018.

p. 51, "if people decide..." "Why Do People Persist in Denying the Moon Landings?"

p. 51, "a coward, a liar..." Brandon Griggs, "Could Moon Landings Have Been Faked? Some Still Think So." *CNN. com*, July 17, 2009, Accessed April 10, 2018.

p. 52, "Unsmudged..." W.H. Auden, *Universification.wordpress.com*, https://universification.wordpress. com/2012/11/04/moon-landing-w-h-auden

p. 52, "We thought, 'We're like the guys...'" Madeline Roth, "Ever Wondered Why the VMA Statue is a Moonman?" *MTV.com*, August 27, 2016, http://www. mtv.com/news/2924701/vma-statue- moonman/ Accessed April 20, 2018.

Select Bibliography

"The Apollo 1 Tragedy." NASA.gov, Digital, https://nssdc.gsfc.nasa.gov/planetary/lunar/apollo1info.html Accessed February 2, 2018.

Chaikin, Andrew. *A Man on the Moon.* New York: Penguin, 2007.

Kennedy, John F. "Address Before a Joint Session of Congress, May 25, 1961," JFKlibrary.org, Digital, https://www.jfklibrary.org/Asset-Viewer/xzw1gaeeTES6khED14P1Iw.aspx Accessed March 3, 2018.

Lovell, Jim, and Jeffrey Kluger. *Apollo 13.* New York: Houghton Mifflin, 1994.

"Why Do People Persist in Denying the Moon Landings?" AirandSpace.SI.edu, April 1, 2010, Digital 8, https://airandspace.si.edu/stories/editorial/why-do-people-persist-denying-moon-landings Accessed March 4, 2018.

Index

About the Author

Rebecca Rissman is an award-winning nonfiction author of more than 300 books. Her work has been praised by *School Library Journal*, *Booklist*, *Creative Child Magazine*, and *Learning* magazine. Rissman especially enjoys writing about American history, aeronautics, and women. She lives in Chicago, Illinois, with her husband and two daughters.